A Reply To The Headlines

A Reply To The Headlines

(Poems, 1965-1970)

Martin Robbins

THE SWALLOW PRESS INC.
CHICAGO

PUBLISHED BY

THE SWALLOW PRESS INC.
1139 SOUTH WABASH AVENUE
CHICAGO, ILLINOIS 60605

LIBRARY OF CONGRESS CATALOG NO. 73-115028

Grateful acknowledgment is made to the following magazines and publications in which many of these poems, several in different versions, first appeared: *The New York Herald Tribune; The Colorado Quarterly; Yankee; Midwestern University Quarterly; The Falmouth Review; Galley Sail Review; Pattersn; The Chicago Tribune; The New York Times; The West Coast Review; The United Church Herald; The Lampeter Herald; The University Review; Film Library Quarterly; Spectrum;* and *New England Review.*

for my father

Contents

I.

II.

III.

IV.

I.

"Good Night, David; Good Night, Chet"

Their facts set tight, their accents clipped,
These analysts of news have taped
The world's corners in labelled cans,
Show us, undaunted, new demands—
With voices collected, faces deadpan.

Instead, I hear the swelling chords
Of old programs, familiar words.
How terror was comfortable then.
The squeaking door swung slowly open—
"Raymond, your host" dared you to fear
Your way through someone's else's Inner
Sanctum. I'd rather hear old time fear
Than what there is and where we are;

But as pinpoint vision fades from sight,
I don't recall that old great light—
Because "good night" won't quite calm us
And I know that now we witness
Just how close we dwell to darkness.

Summer Maneuver

Sudden rain touching summer down
Through leaves, onto pavement, under tires,
Holds a speech deeper than its own sound.
It strafed us. Now time writhes, seeks shelter—
Not fixed warm glass of drifted windows,
Or screens in doors that slam green heat out,
But an arch where pelting sky won't throw
Stored-up hates on us with breath so hot
We can't turn our backs on them. Soft rain
Retakes our city for us. Stand, waiting,
Duck out, step off with no fear, straighten,
Ignore gutters' old, throat-deep warnings.

Unilateral Discussion

The sun ran crimson in all the streets.
My back to the pale wall of twilight,
Shaking off my work's blindfold, I stare.
The reddened faces are informers
On little wars of liberation,
Looking for a way out through reason.

I breathe my orders—in a taxi—
"Look out for that hearse"—thinking I'll see
Stumps that bloom on every corner
With lead. Then I slip through the steel dark.
As time clicks on in its war-head black,
Death, I'll live no limited answer.

On Seeing a Torn Out Coin Telephone

Way to call up quick wishes—
Pizza or chicken—black disaster
Lies there so no one can report
Terror—to try the police once more.

The first thing stupidity says
Rather than face that hollow cell—
Saturday Night at the Movies—hits
My mind, "Get me a mouthpiece."

Wait:

The crazy bell of a drunk laugh.
Instrument, whose nails call for help?
At what man shall I point? Attila
Bludgeons Orion down—while

Civilization, a word too big
For a ten cent call, lies there mute,
Silenced dummy—and who will know
Tonight how many die alone.

Student Roll Call

Twice I called your name in class,
Two days there was a silence.
Then a girl came up and said,
"He's the one, the boy they murdered."

Carotenuti, Gary,
One whose name means "dearly held,"
Name I call again to hold
This time of our rememberance,
How lightly some took you—face
Known on a front page only,
From the matrix of daily
Killing we read, and ignore,
As we turn from each other.
Name I called, not connecting
The poems we're learning
With the prose of violence,
Gary, now forgive my voice.

Yesterday we were to read
"To an Athlete Dying Young."
Today words sound fake and dead.
The only echoes that are strong

Remind us of the dumped thud
Your body made, thrown at night
On stones whose change caused fear's blood
To carve your back with such hate
That I call you now, Gary,
To hold in our memory
What you pumped in a heart,
Made like ours, to make us start
To hear anger understood,
Or choke, echoing the dead
Name I for the last time
Read, whose absence teaches me,
Gary Carotenuti.

"*E Passata La Musica Innocente:*"

Variation on a line of Eugenio Montale

Gaily the music brings
Boylston Street alive—
Hurdy-gurdy all decked
With little flags and glass.

Drum and fife fade before
This spangled melody.
'Play *O Sole Mio.*'
Ah, *musico,* your smile,

Bright as Sicilian noon,
Under black sunglasses,
Grinds: *Vendetta—detta.*
My words are: *Sangue; guerra;*

"*Greggia*"—crowds—as I nod
To the sun through fumes, think
Of Nick the groceryman singing,
Hoarsely, his mother's song,

"I want to go to America,
It's so far away,
America, sta lontano sai"—
'America, like it's our thing.'

Musico, grind your songs;
But sleek, black cars slip by,
Extorting dues from the sun,
"And the innocent music's passed."

Winter Night Scenes

On nights when the moon grips the sky
Quiet and cold as the day's end,
And buildings skeletal as shells
Of some ancient coral city

Cast their thin shadows like the dead;
On nights while fears surface like subs
To launch fire, or glide and nudge
Thoughts of the city gone under when

Our exhausts have melted the ice caps;
On those graveyard nights when my sleep's
Broken, I trudge with my cold feet
Unslippered like a boy, to stand

At the window against the moon.
The frigidaire whines and takes time
Back to my first death. Orion
Strode the sky then, when milk would do

To put me back to sleep, except
One night, my grandfather just gone,
When I stood and stood, small, alone,
Knowing I would leave, restless,

In not so many years. And now,
I stand here with these fears. Chill sky
Of this December seems to say
"Nothing's been reversed;" but cold windows

Still reflect dreams as the huge sky
Holds me here, cautions me to freeze
Anger and fear—and I'm released,
Turning towards stars from machinery.

9

Dissonance: March Winds

Air that clashes brass knives on stone
Cuts me from this sky's exhausts,
And I hear other music: Land
Ploughed up to buffalo grass that stood
At danger's edge; how campfires,
Snorts of horses rode thin on winds
Which, once, only knifed ice of lakes,
Dried ruts, filling air with rich smells.

The thrust of this harsh air pushes me
To the ledge. I hear sirens:
Again night air fills the window
With noises and sounds that echo fears.
The Boston Edison's red clock
Answers the red glare—the city's
Still there, proof against winds. But March
Slashes towards summer, and I smell fires.

Untransfigured Night

A sea-breeze breaks over
Hot apartment roofs.
Planes circle the city,
Dip through night's winking tides.
Windows blink out. Curtains
Waver, sirens wail,
Radio'd voices blare
The latest death tolls.
A baby cries. What words
To cool a day's fevered walls?
Until the search lights pale,
Gone out with the night's red tide,
I walk my creaky floors
To still the squalling hours.

Film Clip

In all the terminals of the world,
The clock reads nearly midnight. Voices
Echo through the arching, hollow domes,
While the tick of terror grips each face
And loudspeakers sound their leaden rain:

Hiroshima, Hiroshima.
                          O,
Mon amour, life, who will comfort you?
Whose hands are untouched by chill metal?

Down pleasure's busy nighttime streets, I
Follow you, wanting to shout through crowds
Of set faces: "It's not too late, there's time."
My affirmation rings tones of will,
Commanding all the animals join
The empty arc of each terminal
Where someone would caress life's face; but,
As clocks boom on, boots of commanders
Echo death's tribunals on marble,
Crisp, uniform, hollow, and deadly.

Postscript to a Czech Movie

Downstairs, just before 6 a.m.,
Across the street, the door opened.
A shadow against yellow light—
Abe the Tailor.
        But all my clocks
Were handless, I was warehousekeeper
For Jewish property, noting
Furs—while his presser warmed up.

Wait! I cried to the dawn while gulls
Wheeled in with vulturous shrieks. Wait!
The man has a buzz in his ear,
Doesn't hear well.
        I won't inform—
But summers I bring ice water, ask
Him to turn down radio'd hate
From the talk shows.
          Wait, my country:
No other men enter his shop;
Only dawn picks up scurriers
Pounding empty messages;
             wait,
It's '68 not '38;
Relatively calm, wind's from the East.
Like a hunted man the presser
Pants—the Fifth Horseman *is* Fear.

Unmailed Letter

Mr. Hoover, have an agent watch
My wastebasket. Please—I can't trust it.
One spring day last year I threw away
A letter from Dr. King. That night
I fished it out and sent some money.
Some time there might be—who knows the pitch—
A letter that's asking help for me.

Mr. Hoover, have an agent check
This mirror. There's a suspicious face
In it, and plots in the medicine
Cabinet—some pills might be poison!
Look at that grinning square—here's the place—
We've got him framed, send an agent quick.
Who knows what this guy will do, he's sick.

Mr. Hoover, have an agent watch
My watch. It's ticking like a time bomb,
Smells of fear and hurry, and its guts
Make words. I've got to break the code, it's
Set for any time now; and—please—I'm
Scared that it just might be me you'll catch.

Mr. Hoover, are you listening?

Letter to an Editor

"The Search of us Southerners is more anguished."
—Ralph McGill, "The Conscience of the South"

Fingers made words right
Because a man's feet knew
Red dust of rural roads,
Because his eyes could scan
A crowd or a courthouse, judge
A face for what it was.

Anger spills in the streets:
Shouts don't stop; change moves slow.
But the gain of one man's span
Has left words to bridge our hate,
Because a man knew a place—
And no fear to tell it right.

Chicago Scene (1952, 1969)

Dawn in my mind.
It betrays no one.
But a man had died.
Ten were needed
So those behind
Could say Kaddish.

Again in dim, chill streets men rush,
In gray coats, again dispossessed.
Carrying velvet bags with stars
Of David woven gold, they rush
Through yellow, shrivelled leaves toward
A rented house, their House of Prayer.

Heavy steps on wood. Then quick words
Of morning worship. Jewish arms bare—
Arms thick as a wagon driver's,
Fragile as a chemist's beaker,
Left arms (some with small blue numbers),
Thonged seven times with black leather.

Thonged near my heart, the black-boxed words
Of the Old Testament rubbed doubt
Of "Thy goodness to Thy creatures."
The Singer studying *Lieder*,
Mumbling lines, I questioned that rewards
And punishments come from our deeds.

And who had died?
At what black hour?
Prayers over,
In slow Yiddish
They told me: A birthday
Was commemorated—

The last fact of a Jew, Polish.
On this dawn I now remember
What a generation's buried.

On a Saturday Afternoon, Late

Wrapped in a sweaty sheet, I woke,
Tried to call back voices from dreams,
Heard the terse announcer—POLAND BLITZED—
And then I heard the cobblestones
Hollow in bone-white sky as we drove
To get fish for Rosh HaShonah.

Now no marvels make dry bones rise,
Sing inner fire that answers death,
Reveal, through pillared cloud, wheels
Whirling to a loud clapping of hands—
Murder's signs are scratched in the sky,
And words still bray from loudspeaker skulls.

Here, a redness lingers. It burns
Clouds like drops of twisted tallow,
Memorial to white Sabbaths
Ended by wine that defined holy
And profane. In what light is now left,
I cup my hand to lingering fire.

17

Through the Rain of Years

Midnight. I squint up from my books.
Light rain: In streets below, the slow,
Wet swish of cars. Their headlights move
Like funerals.
        The past's alive
In a March window which frames hours
Close as the front porch where I arced-out
Kitchen matches with a spring clothes-pin
In rain.
        At this window, the streets
Are wakeful. Black cars move, muffled
As sounds of deaths I've come to know.
And yet the voices on these pages
Are through time beyond those graves.

Fever Chart: Man with Ulcerated Corneas

Until they bandaged up the pain,
Pin-stabs of air wrenched his balance.
He cringed, cursing the appearance
Of probing light, and suppressed cries
Like a child who makes up stories
To sleep easy. He heard them shut
His world's windows, talking about
Transplants and odds.
                He asked for dope.
The needle pierced his mind, and hope
Dropped off beneath the gauzey ache.
Fearing his iris would scar opaque,
He woke before morphine wore off.
Bound by darkness pressing enough
To shake him into thought, he held
The bed's round iron like a pole, stilled
His mind against slashing the air.
Tried to wait, a tightrope walker,
For spotlights to find him.
                No light
Warmed this black chasm, with his sight
Suspended. First a searing torch
Of self pity lit the dark lurch
Of pain. When no beam pierced the days,
His bandaged mind learned that to praise
Distortion lights no soul's dark night,
Just imbalance.
              The chart readers wait.
He serves his time best with lines
That record the night in those signs
Which, in time, become so clear
We see our own health,
                so dear
As light that flashed through gauze like a pin
Whose probing warmed his eyes again,
When doctors, their cautious faces
Bent, reopened his world's places,
Unbandaged the sun, and his pain.

A Reply to the Headlines

Thinking of renewal,
You watch the demolition ball
Slam into greystones. The sounds:
Dim beat of city's prison ground,
Spotlit; compound voices
Through plaster-patched walls; sharp paces
That pound your head with songs
Whose blues beat thumps words out of things.

But survival's design
Still comes from will. The rites of noon
May smash old stone to expose
Wallpaper, and our nights' pose,
A rage at being caught,
Mirrored by ways of the heart's deceit.
But step, not struck by fear,
Off the curbing.
                    Move on and hear
Shoes remind unshaken
Bones that human frames have borne
As much of our world as they've
Made of it. For it's clear to the grave,
Though paths to death are now wide,
The hardest news is buried inside.

20

II.

Song for an August Morning

For once, a Sunday morning sings:
Mind, be still. Too early for bells,
The only piety is light
And leaves. Quiet birds are choiring
Their commonplace. The air, for once
Free of fumes and motorcycles,

Breathes old sweetness. And what one sings
On such an early rising fills
The window not with detailed hate
For cities, but inner space sounding
Out morning's praise. For once
Glad for the ripened miracles

Of air and shadow, here I sing
Not calm that was, or rant of hells
Which might be, or discontent, late
Risen, but a simple humming
To be 'up and doing,' for once
To accept what it is one feels.

Cityscape: West Side Manhattan

Light from the courtyard through blinds.
Its touch on walls with the warm breeze.
Sunday's bed, an island out of time
Whose brows are fanned by careful slaves.
Love on a summer afternoon:
Words disembodied, motion quiet
As the light outside. Noises
Echo the gray place of old buildings.

The snap as a new record drops,
And time returns in the still pause,
Speaks a moment which places us—
Strangers in the city, as all
The foggy days of loss and searching
Touch these walls. Then the calm summer
Breeze rattles the courtyard leaves,
Turns us, silent, to each other.

A Thin Music of September Weather

Late summer, intones a cricket,
A wheeze of temperatures and snow
That fiddles with the mind and chills it.

When will it come, the sickle
Of September's crescent, that pares
The sky down to a bare hill?

What music still plays in the leaves
And brittle stalks? This late summer
Thinking rattles. Its drying sheaves

Burn, as time's unsteady candle,
With small warmth, moves the eye to know
The shadowed music of the fall.

On the Last Day at the Beach

Sand and ocean stretch silence out
To the orange-hooded, lifeguard sun
Huddled to the chilled horizon.
Gulls whirl. A football smacks in the air.
Down the beach, the season's last fire
Grows dim. Before we're pall bearers
Of the spired city's season, here
I turn and find your hand, while wind
Takes our footprints from the sand,
And worlds of sea and sky go mute.

Solstice Morning in Winter Mountains

Stopped one day when the mine shut down,
This wheel that sluiced water through ore
Is fixed against a haze-slowed sun.
The pines are still. The hour holds more
Lead than silver or gold. Snow
Piles the creek. The cold flow is slabbed
With gray, and sun without shadow.
Nobody jumps this claim now grabbed
By winter. No yells that shook aspen
Echo. Silence stills the brain,
Keeps it from the spring wheel that will turn
Snow water back into Clear Creek—gray
With mine tailings. While a truck
Backfires up the canyon as if to say
How much didn't pan out, I look
At a wheel fixed by mountain sun.

Solstice Meditation

What light remains as this year ends?
Few sacred figures move from flames
We fill the night with.—"Happy Times!"—
How words freeze us. What silence bends,

Closing in as darkness stirs fear
That ice will spread with death of the sun?
Small praise remains from warmth once known
As haze fades in this zero hour.

And still, the crusted earth insists
We're free to think beyond this death,
To stir warmth in the air with breath
Constructing April's fragile ghosts

That rise in sun-shaped thoughts to soar
From pine silence of the solstice,
From heart of winter's bone-deep ice,
Through all the arches of the air.

Offering for a Winter Evening

So Blake was right, one can't tell love.
What can I make with words deeper
Than an off hand phrase? I waded
Through words of drift all day,
Thinking of that silence whose breath
Would say my mind's praise.

So I've stomped in, fresh from cold,
The sun's red rim. Headlines' threat
And the city's scrapes fade.
You rise, put out your cigarette.

Look here, love, I want to say
More than some fading cliche
While Babel's towers crumble through dusk.
But my mind's gone dumb,
Thoughts whirl hollow.
"C'me here," I say.

Old Flick

I've offered my amends, even
Confessed I'm no Valentino.

But our words cross, and you
Play get-away music.
I see you, little girl
At your scales, eyes intent.
In my projection room
You flicker, silent star
Of silver screen whose eyes

Reveal the difference between
The things we are and wish to seem.

Eastertide: Rockport, Mass.

On this clear night, a ship's fog horn,
Beyond the bay's lost past, mourns
For hills whose crosses sink in tiered grass.
Our frenzy gives way. Jangle and glass
Fade as stoney brook traces spring's mark
To the sea. As sky grows chill, the stark
Headstones and the huge dim boulders
Surround me. With no clear answer,
Sailor who drinks the moon, I sight
The lines between our stars and fate.

On the Summer Air,

Sounds balance the drowse of hoses
Sputtering slowly their wet arcs.
Mowers whirr safe blades in the park,
Echo green heat, buzz in roses.

Far across grass, shouts call us
To get up, hear the thuds in gloves,
Crack of a bat, while the fielding sun moves
Back on grass—to judge and catch us.

Mid-Summer: Noon Undertones

July sun.
Lions dribble summer's speech.
July haze.
Some leaves fall, though air is still.

City water rusts in pipes.
July heat.
Old men pour out talk in shade.
Clocks mutter.

Boy Floating on a Surfboard

Slow paddler, you make this bay's water
A Pacific to cross. On your stomach,
You drift towards strength, steering the slow fin
That warns me to keep in: Forgotten dreams
Can swamp the sure boats of middle age,
Remind the becalmed that once their minds
Cruised with Magellan. But you seem wiser,
Navigator of your own space. Drift,
Not trying to land, and ride the time,
Good as the sun, easy, slow, and calm.

On Finding an Eye in Houghton Library, Harvard

"Angling is somewhat like poetry . . . he that hopes to be a
good angler must not only bring an inquiring, searching, ob-
serving wit, but he must bring a large measure of hope and
patience, and a love and propensity to the art itself."
— Izaak Walton, *The Complete Angler*

Tired of scanning the minor lines,
With no look over my shoulder
At sovereigns, crowns, fate, or fortune,
I sat back. Autumn to scholars:
So often just a scene through panes.

Finding a new pencil, my hand
Shocked a touch at my heart that came
From my shirt pocket—the same blue kind
I wear fishing. The stab had hit
An eye off my trout rod,
                                    I leaned
To it, saw in its loop, every man
Who's heard the wind riffle water,
Who's stalked trout, held sun still, casting
With arc as far as wrist motion
Can make one's strength into a line.

At the Bass Lake

Casting out his line like a snake
That popped a bass-plug in the weeds,
Smoking, hat brim down like Bogey,
My old man disappeared. He broke

Through bulrushes—far from my dry ground—
By the inlet, and I was sure
He wouldn't be seen again, that smoke
Would hiss out, reeds would close, sound

Would cease. But then he rose, the rod
Bent double, sloshing back to shore,
Landing another large mouth lunker
As he neared the other side.

So miracles continued: Waters
Divided, the sun shone on lakes
Whose time was slow as flooding Nile.
Moses in a pair of waders

Gave his blessing to the simple
Stillness of a May afternoon.
If wilderness was gone, a boy
Could learn the redwings' call, the pull

Of earth to rest, the threat of storms,
Powers of the sun, the water's
Edge—and spiders—thoughts to dig at
Something deeper than the worms.

"The Reel Screamed"

to Elky Stone

When snows of yesteryear drift through days
Whose trips are gone but not forgotten,
What's heard?—open water and open
Sky behind the white, inactive page.

Then a good cast of a true line takes
The stiff time back to afternoons when
Nylon sailed-out. You waited, watching:
A hard strike, and your mind was pulled right
Down into the battle he gave you—
The reel screamed, and you gave him line.

The Tilted Footbridge (Gunnison River)

To my brother, Larry

Held by cables, one on each side,
And a rock jutting from water,
Those old planks would tilt a dare.
You grabbed a cable, looked at the far side.

Passage of danger and adventure,
Twisted by spring floods from past years,
The rickety footbridge pitted fears
Against manhood. If mind was sure

Of foot, you bounced across, your heart
Balanced in your rod. You jumped from stairs,
Walked into shallows and sloshed fears
Downstream as you watched the line float.

The bridge is long gone, caught by wind.
The river's time itself will end,
A dam's coming in—and I who've spanned
Its lesson can't cross it from my mind.

On the Last Trip of the Season

Wading this fall river,
This clear and flat mirror,
I see myself each year
Less a fisherman. But,
Here in midstream, I scout
The water, cast about
Two feet short of what I
Aimed for, then check the sky—
Some hour of light's left me.

The river stills the leaves' fall. My plain thanks
Go to clear water, and the less I think
The more I hear—as if my time's a plank

Bridge above a side creek,
And balance is no trick
Unless I try to look
Through the river's darkest face.
I only ask the grace
To see without grimace,
To learn how years increase
A place, to speak this piece—
Though ice will come to crease.

Afternoon in Concord

Time in the wind takes fall by the arm.
Tall grass in the wildlife refuge twists.
Ducks tip up on cold gray water. Geese
Point the sky towards winter.
                                    On the road
Back in, past house, stacked wood, unraked grass,
A charred Jack O'Lantern stands stern guard.
Voices and leaf smoke hurry me. Leaves
Rattle down the whirling streets.
                                    In town,
I learn history from plaques and walls,
Until branches hold no flame against
Spires that guard the Common, while cold stone
Stands firm as bronzes against dark time.

Winter Pause; Mt. Liberty, N.H.

No crunch of boots,
No wind now moves.
Your breathing slows.
Such stillness holds,
In trees, in sky,
You hear the ice
Return—and time
Speaks the sun's mind
With chill.
           While sound
Ticks snow
Around
You,
      an inner
Voice, like water
In blood, now beats
Each separate
Crystal that takes
The air and sparks
Your heart to move
With the old love—
Climbing again
To the sun's
Motion.

The Claims of Place Give Some Answer

The way that time moves past the spires
And trees of a New England square
Is sung by chill stars—a history
More of grudging work than mystery.
Rebuffed by the stark-white, lean spires,
A cidery autumn sky teeters,
Not willing to come in without
Muttering a few words of regret.
But words won't alter winter's stiff lines,
Or warm the ground beneath the still scenes—
And postcard leaves don't muffle bitter
Voices that sound in our common air.

Night Poem

Winter stars, dim and far. Mist.
The year turns over us. Stalks
In fields, brittle as air, twitch,
Empty as this widened sky.

Insect voices are now still.
The bravest cricket's frozen.
Thin tracks of field-mouse tails,
Ovals of rabbits tell fear.

The great snowy owl waits, white
As time turning, wind that moves
Me to find, wrapped in time,
Those stages of growth before

Hands knew steel. Leaf-bud sheathes
Wait. Cocoons bridge seasons' light.
A small voice in me breathes out
Against stabs of winter stars.

III.

Hours Poetica (By the Sea)

The sky is clear and still. The mind
Turns with will from warming sand
To work words and answer the wind.

Avoid the scan of hectic optic,
And apocalyptic neo-cryptic,
Or onlookers who give myopic
Praise to chance kaleidoscopic.

If the fruit of sunstruck mind
Must mean, then here let's write on sand:
Be, O Muse, more clear than grand.

Self Portrait, 1968

You there with your noncommital look—
Don't open that book—stare, a little.
What you've got to lose, man, is that self
That says 'I've got it made'—and that grin
From those fifty quick sit-ups you pride
Your morning on. Look thoughtful, your eyes
Won't cross future and past, or get all
Those books written which so far only
Have this picture done for the jacket.
Change that smile, think a while, and then,
Poet, come back in five years and see
What time does to words. Figure the odds:
If you don't know what you've got to lose,
Don't sit there composing attitudes.

Watercolor: Beacon Hill

For Leonard Whieldon, 1916-1968

Slanting off the Capitol's gold dome,
Hard against new concrete, light and time
Overlay their patterns. Early spring
Or late fall, the chill sun on buildings
Touches raw umber to the moment,
Which doesn't run to mud as light is spent.
For red-brick sidewalks turn the eye past
Decay to imagine keel and mast
In red sky against spires, thin and pale,
While dashed white in the bay, a late sail.

On the Monets in the Boston Museum of Fine Arts

Season and time
Were Monet's dream.

Stairs climbed with sight of color,
Stand close—hear his labored hours'
Voice: 'Mold living light, Monet;
Learn what the hand gives the eye,
Find those forms that will hold shapes
Resisting the years' footsteps,
And that there is only paint.'

Step back and time will relent.
There—haystacks and cathedrals,
The red flowers in grassy fields,
With a living touch of light
Reveal to eyes a man's sight,
Morning and late, in summer
And winter-crimson hours,

Slow as the sun,
As earth's motion—
In Monet's dream
Of season, time.

Lesson: Artist's Loft

For Robert Wells

The painter, like a monk whose skull
Denies penance, tries his will
As uneasy light pulses on
The white walls of the afternoon.
Removed from rush of common day,
Paint controls flashes of decay.
In unresolved forms, resonance
Of vision holds a stilled defiance
To the fleshy sag of time.
Before light's brush fades in flames
On the city's reddened facade,
His eye moves what his hand will guard.

Greek Procession

(on a painting by Constantine Arvanites)

The painter shapes a dead
Shadow's breath while the words
Sound *Kyrie*. Church flags
Are held in lines against
A flat Byzantine light.

For forty days the Greeks
Still sit in the old ways:
Graveside wails echo
Ashes no longer put
In hair.

Although they know
That Odysseus once clasped
His mother's shade, but held
Ah for his march through Hell,
And not more, still they march.

Flat lines shaped by one man's
Loss makes clear that a grasp
Of spirit can hold light.

In Picasso's "Tragedy,"

Three stand against three:
The figures, father, mother, son;
The chorus, earth, sky, and ocean.
Faced by masks, the boy's mind has turned
Against what's stiff, silent, resigned.

He quavers at waves' bone-white rim.
Blue masks can't answer the lost cry
When time will gouge his eyes' young hymn,
Show his birth was meant as reply
To wordy tide of days that is less
Than dream-speech of endless chorus.

Evening: Museum of Modern Art

The fountains are off,
The traffic's grind goes past.
A still bronze girl,
Untouched by shame or haste,
Her burdens yet
Unborne, waits in the air.
Its calm touches
A man's muscled figure.
And through them speaks
A voice as deep as blood:
The silence of sculpture
Casts its own strong word.

On Drawings by George Grosz

The cigarette's a friendly offer,
Along with more threats—the casual
Sign of power, and the third degree.
What's left to see in that basement cell
"After the Questioning?" The swagger
And upraised fist that power raises
In "Bringing into Conformity."
Check that hand. The prisoner who stands
In "Our Day Will Come," makes that gesture—
To wooden crosses. His other hand,
Weaponless; his temple unravels
The brain's threads as blood drips—whatever
The answer. To study more cases
Just check upstairs—who's not in that file?
The "war-wounded, body-disabled"
Wait in twisted lines, while our fabled
Generals sit for portraits, their eyes
The steel artists of power's lies.

Beyond These Walls Are Endless Rooms

An old master's hand
Shows his search beyond
Life's flesh and time's curve
To find a source of light,
Space and its illusions
Beyond the moment.

Silence, its eyes deep as the mind,
Makes a girl's face firm to thought's touch.
In "Young Woman Reading a Letter,"
Vermeer hears Asia far away,
Past the wave's crash, creak of rigging.
In slow tides of light, her mind
Unfolds the letter with earth's curve

Years beyond. We see
This against a white wall
Whose flat light picks up
Time from two blue chairs
With touch of everyday,
And everlasting.

Liturgy: Dürer's "Hands"

Because there are few words the heart can take,
Because the altar's timbers were bombed in
And hope blew out with the candles and the dust,
Because darkness doubles its wings, shrieking
At structures thought to be shelter, those hands
Still speak. As rubble buries our forms,
And the moment mocks silent gestures,
This strength of veins, doubled against time,
Shaped of bone and flesh by one man's eyes,
Holds us to steady the flame unnamed.

Old Woman Singing in Her Bath

(for Stefanie Fellner, 82)

"Lived through"—is that what the spirit sings?
Your thin voice over running water
Echoes the *Lieder* I sang. Clear eyes
Reflected brooks in Schubert; and when,
In "Poet's Love," I sang to you all
The flowers and sighs, the nightingales,
Bitter tears and children's tales, your lips
Moved with the words of a world destroyed—
Across oceans, deaths of friends, your husband
Murdered by men who sang in German.

If time exacts a truth from the heart
Which music overhears, still keeping
Wonder at May's month, your singing tells me,
Fragile with its splashed rememberings
And thin voice full of recollections,
"Lived through" is what the spirit sings.

Record Notes for a Re-Release

They move us—above the scratched backgrounds.
Caruso sobs in the Clown's passion.
Melba, De Luca, and Chaliapin
Bring lover, villain, and Tsar back to sound,

Tell us their hour with the highest
Power, art that graced the spun-out tone,
Holding time with poise heard less often
Now than in tones a slower day pressed.

Those names that took our hearts are not lost.
But the cup of needles, the turned crank,
The blank side that gave us time to think
Are gone—sound's jacketed in bombast.

You Masters we named the Golden Past,
Give your voices, above those backgrounds,
To us—before we turn the sound
So high all nights touched by sobs are lost.

The College Rooming House Ladies

As quickly twisted door bells
Jar preserves of summer,
These old mates watch at the door,
Take sightings of light bills

In studious eyes, broken
Articles in the quick steps.
With cutlass sweep they open
To boarding their three-decker ships.

Soon all the dim passage doors
Will echo and mock the slam
A man once made. Those pictures
Blanch as the hall clock's chime

Fades off and the powdered wives
Pretend that they can still choose,
Tilting spectacles of lives
Dead set against all booze—

And women. Yet, full sail
On bright September mornings,
They sweep their porch floors, and yell
From quartered decks, halooing

Away their dry, dead time—
While campus bells still jangle
Particles whose bright fall
They watch and try to claim.

Period Piece

Tipsy, that hillside house lurches,
Seven bathtubs over churches.
Salvation couldn't match a hell
Of a good time—for the right people.

While crows watch on shrivelled branches,
No Feds close in on their hunches.
No ghosts stagger out to speak
The house easy. I throw a rock

At its condemned grin that misses,
Just rattles like all the passes
Time made, finally won by bones—
Yet it makes seven skips on a lake of gin.

Some Land Not Taken

(for an Interstate Road)

An old, thin ghost, the gray frame house
Was perched above a truck-farm road.
Boards had x'd out all the windows—
Comic strip eyes waiting for nights
When jazz speaks time easy. G'bye,
Twenties, no more gin medicine,
Top hat silver-lined with good times.
Men came, metal hats on their heads,
Built an asphalt plant, lined earth black—
But left the house, a cock-eyed hat.

On the C.B. & Q.: The Denver Zephyr

Hollow with the click of speed on track,
Going East, all night, quick wheels fading.
Crossing-towns, shacks, farmhouse lights told
Such stories before fading beneath
Heat lightning that swept the prairie night.
Who could say what grew in that hot night?

What the voices said at Council Bluffs
Were quick words, with hard kisses, before
Duffel bags were shouldered like courage,
And a hot lantern swung its white arc
To wave the train into Iowa
While diesel horn blared against distance.

Two hours from Chicago, light brought
A green morning and gray frame houses,
Crossing-towns peopled with stay-at-homes
Who never notice the passengers—
Come from Colorado rich with gold,
Eating fancy eggs in the diner,
Buffalo-shooting boys at windows,
Riding overland back from frontiers.

Streets of Chicago, the pillared El,
Time everywhere—high on corner clocks,
On faces whose eyes hurried and dodged
In patchy light where crowds made feet move
Down sidewalks. Police whistles' *Ph-whee-o*
Paced the hours—
                          left behind at Five
From Union Station. Then Aurora,
Green land again. The Mississippi
Crossed, Iowa towns flashed by, and
Rust-red boxcars' EVERYWHERE WEST. Now
The roads merge and passengers will be
A thing of the past, the trainmen say.

But I, who overheard the sleeping voices
From hills of each deaf graveyard, know
The "Q" always linked us with the past;
And remember how twilght faded,
A golden spike joining rails and sky,
Across the plains—and then the wait
At the window until the moon caught
The wide Missouri Indian-still.

Four Lectures on the Elements as Air, Fire, Water and Earth

I. Smoke

The sun which made our air
Now hangs fire two hours
Too soon in thick red sky.
Smoke is our element now,
And air's a beast we tame,
Circling the collar tight.

If that's remote—look: Haze
From big steel burns light orange;
Their chimneys cough flame
While freeway tail lights spit blood,
And the trapped sky's red mouth
Turns to gnaw on itself.

II. Light

The pulse of quasars deepens space
Beyond what we thought was limitless,
Leaves us to our own devices
In this green, breathing time and place.

It warms us safe to see how high
Our brains can reach. For floods so deep
The rocks hold bones swirl below sleep
And take our hopes beyond the eye.

We touched lines of order from star
To star and named them. Now we watch
Bands out of time whose dim blue touch
Moves far past our one white star.

Yet the atom's truth is just. Force
Fused in the sun's furnace will burn
A length whose spectral light won't turn
To dust the vision of endless space.

III. Blood

Stream of our time,
History's name,
Ocean's memory,
Pride, patrimony,
Speak, blood.
Untwist your red

Shelves from the glaciers' path,
From the tigers' keen teeth.
Slowly through the dumb forms
You rose to speak bones warm;
Still, your dumb truth carries
And heals, spills, miscarries,

And follows blind
Through time's red mind.

IV. Bones

The claims of earth are paid with bones.
At their short fall, the ready soil,
Opened to cold and saddened speech,
Takes what time and the sea once owned.

History piles its own mounds up.
The tools are left beside the bones.
The gaze of empty sockets glares
Out of time: So much silence

Asking the skull of man be learned
Before it bleaches in history's
End, and asking praise for forms
Dust alone never gathered.

Earth, my answer to your sad words,
Turned in the sun's mad season, held
Mute, is to voice wonder like a rock
Skipped light years across dark cosmos.

IV.

A Book of Hours for the Twentieth Century

Matin (After the Reopening of the Vienna State Opera, 1955) for Rudi
   Fellner

Achtung! Achtung! falls on *Opern Platz.*
Just some loudspeakers, moving traffic
Of diplomatic cars. But echoes
Go deeper than Beethoven's *Fidelio*—
Thud of American bombs, the screams
From skulls which German boots kicked aside.

Between acts: *"Küss die Hand*—strings again—
"Wienerblut, our waltzes!" Then outside
Again, I see black shrouds in shadows,
And ask, accompanist who taught me
The Beethoven you'd learned in *Wien,*
What words can now be sung in chorus?

Freiheit, Freiheit—Freedom? Past midnight,
The wind mutters, *"Kauf nicht bei Juden."*
A church bell echoes a silence as deep
As when my eyes were struck by white robes
Worn by the chorus, your townspeople,
Whose German froze me in a blaze of light.

Lauds (Sunrise, Beacon Hill)

Across Back Bay, the village of Cambridge
Patches some windows on darkness. My books
Keep old worlds from silence.
                              Pre-dawn touches
Sky. Gray clouds emerge. Blue highway-lights still
Shine. This world grows clearer.
                              Of such a sky
The firmament was made. Patches of light

Streak the gray. Steeples, leaves, slate roofs, chimneys,
Red bricks pick-up light.
                                    Glass flames high buildings.
I close my books, whose words now sing: "Give praise;
The sun's come back around the earth's dark side."

Prime (Kaddish Prayer, Florence, 6 a.m.)

Beyond piles of crated produce,
A thick, high wall, locked gates—refuge
Of the Jews.
                        Inside, silence. Names
On plaques. Here, the murdered remain.
Renato Cohen, the priestly line
Has been defiled.
                              I, a Levite,
In your synagogue, pour out words,
Water to cleanse your hands—the world.

Terce (Chicago, 9 a.m.)

Wind off Lake Michigan.
Busy in morning sun,
The city shrugs at heat.
The Loop fills with late feet,
In cool shadows, we trace,
A black man, and I, grace
Of steel. Riveting noise—
Sparks shower. In his face
Chicago's South Side burns,
As cops whistle traffic on.

Sext (Requiem, Venice, Midday)

Through winter fog, muffled as death's
Procession—crepe-decked gondolas.

Priest in the first, and family.
Next, the casket, flowers. The wake
Proceeds: Then it holds a friar's
Reflection——he sweeps chill stone.
His lips move——*give us rest*——as sun

Burns through fog——*give us light*——and
He gestures black procession out
Towards the cemetery island's palms.

Nones (In a garden, West Side New York, 3 p.m.)

Summer trees sag in the heat.
The voice of the TIMES repeats
The losses of American
Saturday afternoons.
More news of foreign squabbles
Fades into the courtyard squall.

"Amor," a wobbly high C
From the eternal Mimi
Of 2B (who never goes
Off with anyone) echoes
Her grand opera's delusions,
Doesn't move the loveless sun.

Vespers (Rome, Afternoon Tour)

Tone of empire; forum of bones;
Tongue descended from clipped grandeur,
Dulle to brash dialect—"*Ashpett'*."
What do you "wait" for, hilled city?

Staccato as the scooters, *"ti"*
Breaks down time; the formal "you"
Recedes, leaving debris.
                    "E qui . . ."
"And here," barbarian, Rome scorns
In its own tongue. Grotto'd skulls
Utter more death than words have told.

From silence, stairways lead the ear
To babble where no law's proclaimed,
No chariot wheels strike sparks on stone.

Red haze touches pines, rush
Of fountains veils the twilight, bells
Push gray marble—*"Ashpett'"*—"I wait."
Hilled city, what do you wait for?

Compline (Nightfall, Harvard)

A thumb-worn book with rubric
Glow burning on the margin,
Day has closed over the Charles.
Time has paled from banks and sky;
Bells of St. Paul's towers speak,
Denying light has fallen.

Then a crescent moon captures
The hour, skimming in single-scull
Through thoughts calmed only by will—
Its wake cold music of stars.

A Tenor's Vocalise to the Morning, in the Century of the Holocaust

(A dramatic monologue for reading, stage, or film)

> On a small, folding kitchen table are a
> pitch-pipe (round kind), a score of the
> Verdi Requiem (Schirmer edition), a
> copy of the TIMES, a round shaving mir-
> ror (the kind with standers), and flashy,
> but not really expensive sport coat.
> [Notes: Tape can be used if reader/actor
> doesn't sing; the stanza is an eight line
> one.]
> The tenor stretches and groans.

Oh. That damn party:

> Bows as if meeting someone.

"Mrs. Morency,

Our tenor." Or was it Mountmorency?

It'll be a damn cold day in hell when

Anyone mounts that battle-ax (*Waves arms*) "Hiya-ta-ho!"

> He looks at the Times.

One lousy line, and I was great. Oh, Christ,

Don't they get it—you're alive when you're singing,

Not at their parties.

> Checks watch.

Nancy was mad;

Putting her in a cab wasn't enough.

> Puts both hands on his diaphragm, in-
> hales deeply, watching his hands being
> pushed out, then sings, on one tone—
> sustained:

"Oh."

> Pats his stomach.

Fifty this morning, old man. 'Ya wanna

Feel my diaphragm muscles, baby?' (*Inhales, sings:*) "Ah."

> Adjusts his tie, singe; [The "hung"
> is sustained, the 'ah' short]

"Hung-ah." Will I have enough this morning?

Christ, at ten!

Sings, pulling diaphragm muscle in
with each syllable:
"Ha. Ha, ha, ha, ha, ha."
When I was a baritone, I loved that laugh—
"Heaven's old fable." That's it, Iago.

He pulls his jaw as he pronounces,
the next word [Yyyy-a!]
Ja!

Speaks, operatically:
"E poi? La morte—ē il nulla."
And then—death, and nothingness.

Sings Iago's laugh (from his "Credo"
in Verdi's Otello.
"Ha, ha, ha, ha."
Breathes deeply, putting hands at his
ribs, checking to see that the breath
pushes them out. Sings, on one tone:
"Eee"—zey there.

Rubs his cheeks, smiles.
Fill the resonators: "Eee"—
Plur-eee-bus."

Opens the score, blows "E" on pitch pipe,
sings the tenor (chorus) entrance [p. 2]:
"Requiem."
Picks up score, turns to solo tenor en-
trance [p. 9], takes deep breath, exhales
it, blows "A", sings:
(If filmed, camera might show his actual
entrance at the peformance, with or-
chestra, etc.)
"Ky-ri-e."
Hold it.

Puts score down; picks up mirror;
Grabs jaw, nervously

Jaw's a little tight. Tongue loose—breathe. (*Does.*)
As he breathes, he opens his arms, as if
breathing a mountainside of flowers, eyes
closed, then pats on stomach (as NOT
to assume a crucified look).

64

What would they say if they knew the struggle
With this mach-"eee"-n?

*Turns head from side to side as he sings
the "ee." Blows "A" again, sings on one
tone:*
"Pee-pay; pee-pay; blah."
Yes, Mr. Treasurer, 'blah.' (*Sings*) "Pee-pay, blah."
You think your green's as good as a High C?—
When your heels vibrate.

Blows "f" and sings:
"Una furtiva . . ."
Checks watch.
Hey! Nine-thirty!

Pats the score.
The score's marked.
*Blows the pitch pipe (G#), sings, on
one tone:*
"Aeternam."
Could I fake it today? Not with Verdi.
He didn't. Walked down that street between them,
Their guns were cocked. He stopped them. He believed.

*He whistles "liberty" motif from Verdi's
Don Carlo, then sings a tenor phrase from
a duet from that opera [p. 24 Ricordi
edition, top stave]:*
"Liberta."

He looks into the mirror.
And you? What do you believe?
Sings Iago's opening of the "Credo":
"Credo in un Dio crudel." Cruel God.

*This bothers him. He looks in the mirror
again; down to the TIMES; then, distant-
ly, as if recalling another performance,
sings from Bach's B Minor Mass:*
"Credo

In unum Deum."

Loosens jaw, lightly with fingers.
Day, day, day.
Slaps the TIMES.
Great night. But today, I'm not myself—scared.

*He opens the Verdi score to the tenor
solo [p. 71], reads:*
"Ingemisco tamquam reus,"
I tremble as before a judge.
No. I'm ready—and what tenor
Doesn't want to sing this solo:
*Blows "C" on pitch pipe, sings:
(Can be filmed—if so, score is in black
cover.)*
"Ingemisco tamquam reus."
But feel submission?—Heaven's throne!
God, every time I get depressed
He flips to basso solo p. 75.
I think the bass's words—flames, hell—
Blows "B," sings:
"Confutatis meledictis,
Flammis acribus abdictis,
Voca me cum benedictis."
"Call me forth with thine elected."
Benediction; maledication (*smiles toothily*)
So long as they praise my diction.
No.
He slams score shut.
 What's behind all my 'knowledge'?
God, it's a game. You get a cue,
And then you're off on some grand expression,
Or some intimate confession; but where
Do you stand, singer? And what do you think?
He looks at cover of the score.
I think I've got a few good years left, five,
Maybe, when I can still move them with sheer
Beauty—and then you finally go to hell—
Like all the singers, to follow their voices,
Which went to hell years ago.
Sings, jokingly:
"Confutatis."
Looks at his watch.
There's time to walk. Some thought might come to me
On the way.

Picks up sport coat.
Yeah, sure, in an even tread
Like they walked to the gas chambers.
                    He tosses score on the table.
                                        Listen,
Verdi, did you that they sang your piece,
In a camp where they 'detained' children—'bad
Children'—they were Jewish—and the grownups
Gave *one* performance of your *Requiem?*
                    He struggles into his coat, as if being
                    grappled with.
And what should I sing? I sing anything—
In Cathedrals, Temples, recital halls,
Concert stages—"there's the tenor, true voice,"
They say. Maybe sometime . . .
                    He buttons his coat; picks up score.
                    . . . to the spirit
Of Tremblinka I should just make silence,
Walk out and make silence—and be ruined.
Not out of guilt. One singer can't walk
Between six million voices.
                    Looks at score, sings the "Liber Scriptus"
                    [p. 36]:
"Liber scriptus proferetur,
In quo totum continetur . . ."
                    Puts his hand on it, like swearing on a
                    Bible, says
"When the Creature, sorrow-smitten,
Rises before a judge." "Ingemisco
Tamquam Raus." I can almost see it,
A page of history that closes shut,
In ashes, "mundus judicetur"—
"And behold the doom-book written."

What did they die for? Silence. A silence
That all my grand opera is empty.
"Father, I'm in doubt," that's what King Phillip
Said to the Grand Inquisitor.
                    Knocks on the table, 1-2-3, like the chords
                    announcing the Inquisitor's entrance in
                    Don Carlo.

                                        Well, I'm not.
The air these lungs needs to sing such music
Holds the dust of bones. Then—it was just flesh.
In Spain, the Kol Nidre was said to tell God
The vows they'd had to make were not vows.
Confess and be forgiven? If my voice
Could speak for anyone, I'd sing their formula:
                    He sings.
                    Possible shot of a deathcamp service
"Kol Nidrei, ve-e-so-ray, ve-cha-re-may . . ."
Six million times, not three times.
                              But, I sing opera.
Don Carlo dies for the tenor, for liberty . . .
                    Sings, Don Carlo [p. 245, 3d. stave].
"Morra per te."
                    Looks at watch; smoothes jacket; throws
                    out chest.
            Well, old man, when baritones
Die for tenors, that's the composer's fault.
As for the rest . . .
                    He opens the score.
      . . . That entrance, I won't be late.

                    He opens to the alto chorus cue, p. 8,
                    then comes in with the tenor solo
                    entrance:
"Lu-ce-at e"—"Ky-ri-e"—it's on pitch,
But my jaw. Like there's a weight, it's so tight.
Yeah. The weight of his skull, that tenor they heard,
And then murdered.
                    Pulls his jaw down with both hands,
                    gently [which is also like holding a
                    skull], and sings the opening of the Verdi
                    Requiem:
                    "Re-qui-em ae-ter-nam."
                    He knocks on the table in the rhythm of
                    the bass drum from the Requiem's Dies
                    Irae.
"Dies irea," day of wrath, "dies illa."
Auschwitz, Hiroshima, Nagasaki—

You, the audience, feeling safe, in white gloves,
It's you they select, "solvet saeclum in favilla . . ."

You're next.
                              He flips pages to his solo [p. 73], *blows*
                              a "B flat," sings:
              "Inter oves locum praesta,
Et ab haedis me sequestra" . . . (*bitterly*): "With thy
Sheep, Oh Lord, deign to rate me, from the
Wicked separate me—"
                              Slugs his jaw with a clenched fist.
                              Got to get out!
They'll be waiting for me. For you? They said
He was young, that tenor.
                              He looks down at the mirror on the table.
                    Not yet! My roles,—
I want people to hear me—hear and feel—
A human spirit's left, not just ashes.
                              He turns to the "Lachyrmosa" [p. 87],
                              reads the translation in his score (which
                              is Swinburne's, not the Schirmer.)

"Prayer, like flame with ashes blending,
From my crushed heart burns ascending;
Have Thou care for my last ending."
                              Blows "F" on pitch-pipe, sings:
"Lachrymosa dies illa,
Qua resurget ex favilla
Judicandus homo reus—
Huic ergo parce Deus."
                              Puts pitch-pipe down, touches jaw, says:
"Prayer, like flame with ashes blending . . ."
                              Looks at his watch.
                                        Oh, Christ!
Well, if I run, it won't hurt my breathing.
                              Puts score under his arm.
Come on, man, you'll be hearing their
Footsteps on the stairs. (*Half serious*) But I'm not political.
                              Knocks on the table, with the Grand In-
                              quisitor rhythm: [1-2-3]

History, the Grand Inquisitor, dressed
In the blood-red robes of our "solutions."

Opens the Verdi Requiem to the last
page, sings:
"Lord, deliver my soul from the doom
Of eternal death in the great day
Of judgment. Libera me."

Shuts score quickly, and leaves for the
rehearsal.